WHERE'S BORIS?

Illustrated by
Wan at Monkey Feet

Copyright © Orion 2014

The right of Orion to be identified as
the author of this work has been asserted in accordance
with the Copyright, Designs and Patents Act 1988.

This edition first published in Great Britain in 2014 by Orion
an imprint of the Orion Publishing Group Ltd
Orion House, 5 Upper St Martin's Lane,
London WC2H 9EA
An Hachette UK Company

10 9 8 7 6 5 4 3 2 1

A CIP catalogue record for this book is available
from the British Library.

ISBN: 978 1 409 15353 5

Printed in China

The Orion Publishing Group's policy is to use papers that
are natural, renewable and recyclable and made from
wood grown in sustainable forests. The logging and
manufacturing processes are expected to conform to
the environmental regulations of the country of origin.

Every effort has been made to fulfil requirements with
regard to reproducing copyright material. The author
and publisher will be glad to rectify any omissions at
the earliest opportunity.

www.orionbooks.co.uk

INTRODUCTION

Welcome to the wonderful oik-spurning, mop-quiffing, champagne-quaffing, totally spiffing world of Boris Johnson.

Follow BoJo's adventure roaming the glorious streets of London (the greatest city on earth!), around the world to far-flung Beijing and back in time to the golden days of the Bullingdon Club. Your noble mission is to find Boris in every picture – he is the only gent to be wearing a blue rosette.

For those of you with a keener eye, there are even more bits and bobs to spot. Go through the 'What to Find on Each Page' section on the following pages to tick off all the extra nuggets of search-and-find joy. Then give yourself a jolly good pat on the back if you can relate the object to a blustering Boris gaffe, spectacular triumph or particularly memorable comment.

To the victors go the spoils – so keep your eyes peeled, go forth and find Boris!

WHAT TO FIND ON EACH PAGE

'Park Life' – Victoria Park

- [ ] An apology letter – this time it's addressed to the people of Liverpool (RE: The Beatles issue)
- [ ] A piggybacking couple
- [ ] 'Someone get me a rope…'. Find a coil of rope to rescue Boris
- [ ] '…or a stepladder!' Find a stepladder to rescue Boris

- [ ] And Mitt Romney thought we wouldn't be ready for the Olympics! Ha! Can you see a hint of him *floating* around?
- [ ] A 'Boris' bike
- [ ] An Elvis lookalike
- [ ] A man waving a Union Jack
- [ ] Someone talking on their mobile

'Game On' – Olympic Stadium

- [ ] An apology letter – this time it's addressed to the people of Portsmouth
- [ ] An Olympic medal going spare
- [ ] A water cannon – in case the crowd get a little too rowdy
- [ ] A gong
- [ ] Are those women playing volleyball? Oh no, it's just some glistening wet otters with a beach ball

- [ ] And the water from those wet otters 'is plashing off the brims of the spectators' sou'westers'. Find these yellow-coated onlookers
- [ ] Two children seated on adult shoulders
- [ ] A heart banner
- [ ] A royal visit! Find the Queen

'Getting the Chop' – At the Barber Shop

- [ ] An apology letter
- [ ] A super-strength golden comb – it's what a precious head of hair deserves
- [ ] A saxophone player
- [ ] It's Boris' busking pal – dreadlock-haired Newton Faulkner!
- [ ] A dapper young fellow, with his jacket flung over his shoulder
- [ ] 'WHERE'S YOUR BROOM? WHERE'S YOUR BROOM?!' chant the crowds. Find the Broom – Boris's weapon of choice for any heroic act of riot clean up
- [ ] A pink lady being swept off her feet
- [ ] A man working on his laptop
- [ ] Someone doing a handstand

'Wiff-waff – Ping-Pong Arena

- [ ] An apology letter – this time it's addressed to Papua New Guinea (RE: cannibalism)
- [ ] The rules of wiff-waff
- [ ] Purple-shirted man having the time of his life
- [ ] A time-travelling 19th Century wiff-waff spectator
- [ ] Original wiff-waff bats
- [ ] At least one old English dining table
- [ ] The ping-pong challenge to end all ping-pong challenges – Pippa Middleton versus Boris Johnson. Can you see her in that oh-so-famous white dress?
- [ ] A suited man jumping for joy
- [ ] A brown handbag thrust in the air with gay abandon

'On your Bike!' – Piccadilly Circus

- [ ] An apology letter
- [ ] Once spotted on a personal Boris motor – an 'I heart Scotland' bumper sticker
- [ ] A group of beer-drinking 'oiks'
- [ ] Grey-haired couple holding a placard
- [ ] A green bike helmet
- [ ] Someone about to be pickpocketed
- [ ] Not just for tourists – can you see Kate and Wills riding in a rickshaw?
- [ ] A pigeon on a post
- [ ] Man in a white 'wife-beater' tank top

'The Tube' – London Underground

- [ ] An apology letter – this time it's addressed to the hoteliers of London
- [ ] An oyster card (the little blue card that allows you to roam the city)
- [ ] The London Evening Standard newspaper
- [ ] A certain someone's upcoming book poster
- [ ] One of the world famous tube buskers
- [ ] Do you know the cost of a pint of milk? Find a poster for a pretty expensive estimate
- [ ] A Tory suitcase – complete with rosette
- [ ] Four suits in hard hats
- [ ] A street entertainer statue

'The Glass Gonad' – City Hall

- [ ] An apology letter – this time it's addressed to Malaysian students (RE: the marriage issue)
- [ ] A smart gent on stilts
- [ ] A cool quarter of a million quid for a second job is apparently 'chicken feed' – can you see the real chickens and their paltry pickings here?
- [ ] A sword juggler
- [ ] Sometimes found debating in City Hall, Russell Brand is wandering the crowds outside
- [ ] Arch rival Ken Livingstone
- [ ] A Labrador Retriever
- [ ] A Latin textbook
- [ ] Would you hug one? A group of 'hoodies'

'The Forbidden City' – Beijing

- [ ] An apology letter
- [ ] 'The Beijing Beatles' tribute band – a special performance for the visiting mayor
- [ ] A Brompton bike
- [ ] Handed over with dignity – the Olympic torch
- [ ] A man with a scroll
- [ ] A pair of red eyes
- [ ] Tourist group taking a selfie
- [ ] A child in a pink hat
- [ ] A lady in traditional Chinese dress, complete with purple umbrella

'No.10' – Downing Street

- [ ] An apology letter – this time it's addressed to the London Irish community (RE: lefty crap)
- [ ] Boris is always hanging out with Babs Windsor of *Eastenders'* landlady fame. Can you see her?
- [ ] And what about the iconic Queen Vic bust from the TV show's pub?
- [ ] A choir

- [ ] It's always a bit of a scrum near the PM's house, but will Boris pick up the rugby ball? Find it in this picture
- [ ] Old Etonian stripy blazer
- [ ] David Cameron himself
- [ ] A TV crew's microphone
- [ ] A dark horse

'Posh Nosh' – The Bullingdon Club

- [ ] An apology letter
- [ ] That strawberry dessert delight – a serving of Eton mess
- [ ] A magnum of champagne
- [ ] 2 purple bottles
- [ ] A roast swan
- [ ] A roll of bin bags – necessary if you are likely to vomit at the table (an almost certain side effect of drunken foppery)

- [ ] A rifle
- [ ] 6 security guards – not taking any chances with these guys
- [ ] A club member perusing the extensive wine list

'Park Life' – Victoria Park

Tally ho! Everyone is in an Olympic mood and having a good old frolic around Victoria Park. The sun is shining, the balloons are out and people are flying through the air. So come on, what are you waiting for? Get your national flags out, wave them with vigour and start finding Boris!

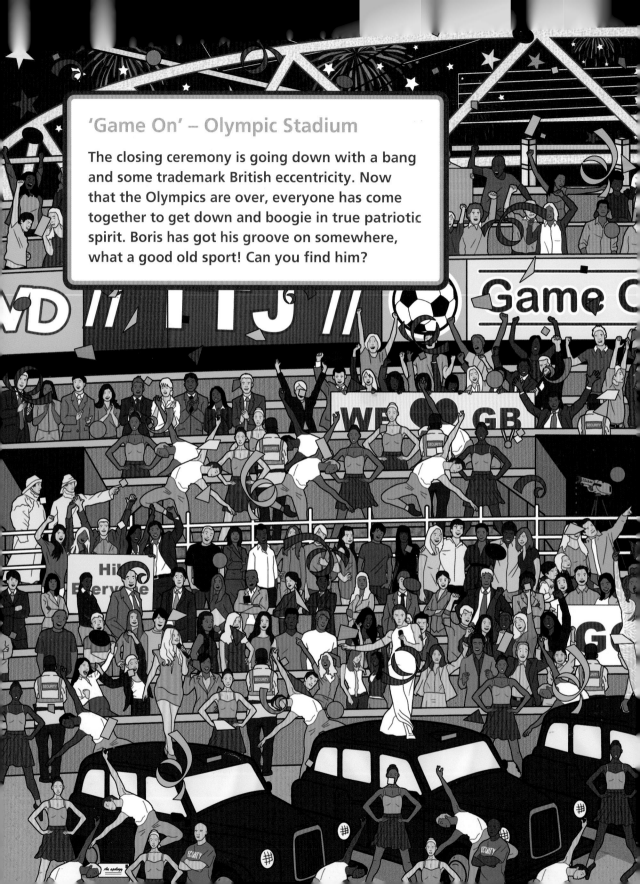

'Game On' – Olympic Stadium

The closing ceremony is going down with a bang and some trademark British eccentricity. Now that the Olympics are over, everyone has come together to get down and boogie in true patriotic spirit. Boris has got his groove on somewhere, what a good old sport! Can you find him?

'Getting the Chop' – At the Barber Shop

Regular trims are the secret to a perfect crop of messy mop hair – as Boris well knows. Amongst the throng around the barbers on this busy London street can you get a glimpse of Boris and his famous unruly blonde hairdo?

LOOKING For A Job?

'Wiff-Waff' – Ping-Pong Arena

It's coming home, it's coming home, it's coming ... wiff-waff's coming home! A game like ping-pong was played on the dinner tables of Victorian England and now they're all at it again. Boris is keen to join in with tapping the balls – but can you spot him amongst the crowd?

'On your bike!' – Piccadilly Circus

Pip pip! It's the great Boris bike rally! Cheer on at the sidelines as the cyclists whizz around the statue of Eros in Piccadilly Circus. Don't let the bright lights, tooting cars and downright joviality distract you – Boris is here somewhere and you need to track him down.

'The Tube' – London Underground

The London Underground is a special place. Face to face with fellow passengers, sharing close personal space and awkward silence, you can be sure to travel in style on the tube. Boris Johnson is taking a ride on this fine means of public transport – can you see where he is?

'The Forbidden City' – Beijing

Never one to miss a photo opportunity, Boris is visiting the Forbidden City in Beijing. He's on a trade mission but he can't help charming (and baffling) the locals. But in this bustling and highly populated country, he's got himself lost. Can you see him shuffling about?

'No.10' – Downing Street

Plebeians, beware! It's the usual media scrum outside Number 10 and Boris is ready to catch the ball. But is he waiting in the wings or in the running up front? Search for Boris to find out!

'Posh Nosh' – The Bullingdon Club

'Buller, buller, buller!' Champagne quaffing, caviar guzzling, top and tails wearing members of the Oxford all-male drinking society are having another one of their memorable dinners. Somewhere in amongst the toffishness and twittishness is Boris – can you spot him?

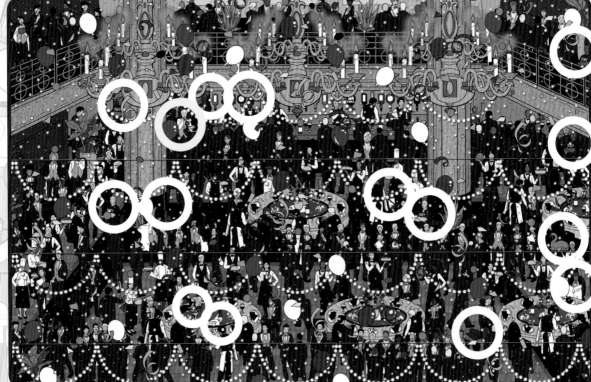